ICONS

PEDRO PASCAL

BY KATHLEEN CONNORS

Enslow PUBLISHING

Please visit our website, www.enslow.com.
For a free color catalog of all our high-quality books, call toll free 1-800-398-2504 or fax 1-877-980-4454.

Library of Congress Cataloging-in-Publication Data
Names: Connors, Kathleen, author.
Title: Pedro Pascal / Kathleen Connors.
Description: Buffalo, New York : Enslow Publishing, 2026. | Series: Icons | Includes index.
Identifiers: LCCN 2025001666 (print) | LCCN 2025001667 (ebook) | ISBN 9781978544550 (library binding) | ISBN 9781978544543 (paperback) | ISBN 9781978544567 (ebook)
Subjects: LCSH: Pascal, Pedro--Juvenile literature. | Actors--United States--Biography--Juvenile literature. | LCGFT: Biographies.
Classification: LCC PN2287.P269 C66 2026 (print) | LCC PN2287.P269 (ebook) | DDC 791.4502/8092 [B]--dc23/eng/20250120
LC record available at https://lccn.loc.gov/2025001666
LC ebook record available at https://lccn.loc.gov/2025001667

Published in 2026 by
Enslow Publishing
2544 Clinton Street
Buffalo, NY 14224

Designer: Tanya Dellaccio Keeney
Editor: Kristen Rajczak Nelson

Photo credits: Cover, p. 25 DFree/Shutterstock.com; p 4 holly_molly/Shutterstock.com; pp. 5, 7, 13 WENN Rights Ltd/Alamy Images; p. 9 Image Press Agency/Alamy Images; p. 11 Everett Collection Inc/Alamy Images; pp. 15, 16, 23 Album/Alamy Images; p. 17 AFF/Alamy Images; p. 19 PictureLux/The Hollywood Archive/Alamy Images; p. 20 Sipa USA/Alamy Images; p. 21 BFA/Alamy Images; p. 27 Entertainment Pictures/Alamy Images; p. 29 Imago/Alamy Images.

Printed in the United States of America

CPSIA compliance information: Batch #CSENS26: For further information contact Enslow Publishing, at 1-800-398-2504.

Contents

Words in the glossary appear in **bold** the first time they are used in the text.

Chile Born

Pedro Pascal was born José Pedro Balmaceda in Chile on April 2, 1975. His family left South America to live in Denmark and then the United States when he was a baby. They lived in San Antonio, Texas, and then southern California.

ICONIC!

Pedro's mother died when he was 24 years old. He started using her last name as his stage name to honor her. He also found it was easier for Americans to say!

Learning to Act

As a kid, Pedro loved going to the movies. He knew from a young age that he wanted to be an actor. While living in California, Pedro went to a **performing** arts high school. Then, he went to New York University (NYU) to study acting.

ICONIC!

Pedro met actress Sarah Paulson while at NYU. They are still friends today!

TV Time

Pedro graduated, or finished classes, from NYU in 1997. He stayed in New York City and tried to find work as an actor. But Pedro mostly worked other jobs, such as waiting tables. In 1999, Pedro moved to Los Angeles, California. He booked his first acting job!

ICONIC!

One of the first acting jobs Pedro got was on the '90s hit TV show Buffy the Vampire Slayer.

SCREEN
ACTORS
GUILD
AWARDS
AFTRA
FLIX

During the early 2000s, Pedro appeared on many other TV shows including *Homeland, Law & Order, Nurse Jackie*, and *The Good Wife*. He was glad to be working, but he hadn't gotten any big breaks—yet.

ICONIC!

Pedro later said of this time in his life: "The smallest of ***opportunities*** *kept me going. So much so that I* ***resolved*** *to struggle until I couldn't walk anymore."*

On Stage

Pedro acted in many plays during this time too. He mostly performed around New York City. Pedro played Horatio in *Hamlet* in a Washington, DC, theater too. However, even when he performed off-Broadway, the jobs didn't pay very well.

ICONIC!

*Off-Broadway is **professional** theater in New York City. It's known for showcasing plays that are inventive and imaginative.*

A Breakthrough!

Sarah Paulson helped Pedro with money sometimes. Then, she helped him get his **audition** for *Game of Thrones* directly to one of the **showrunners**. Pedro got the part of Oberyn Martell, a character who dies a bloody death. It aired in 2014—and Pedro finally got noticed!

Pedro as Oberyn Martell

ICONIC!

When Pedro read the part of Oberyn Martell, he thought he was perfect for the part.

Pedro's **career** took off. He starred in the Netflix show *Narcos* from 2015 to 2017. He acted alongside Matt Damon in the movie *The Great Wall* in 2016. He even got to play the bad guy in *Kingsman: The Golden Circle* in 2017.

Pedro in Narcos

Matt Damon

ICONIC!

Pedro speaks Spanish. He got to use this skill on Narcos.

Donning the Helmet

Pedro started being offered parts he didn't need to audition for. When Pedro was asked to talk about *The Mandalorian* with showrunner Jon Favreau, Jon already knew he wanted Pedro in the part. *The Mandalorian*, starring Pedro as Din Djarin, came out in 2019.

Pedro in The Mandalorian

ICONIC!

Jon Favreau told Variety *in 2020 that Pedro "feels very much like a classic movie star."*

The Mandalorian was a huge hit! It made Pedro a star, even though his face is covered for most of the show. The second season of *The Mandalorian* came out in 2020. Then, a third season came out in 2023.

ICONIC!

Pedro played Maxwell Lord in Wonder Woman 1984. *It came out on Christmas Day in 2020.*

Icon Status

Next, Pedro took on another **iconic** role: Joel in *The Last of Us*. The show was based on a popular video game of the same name. Again, the people making the show had Pedro in mind for the part. The show was a big hit when it came out in 2023!

ICONIC!

Pedro hosted Saturday Night Live *in 2023. He was* ***nominated*** *for an Emmy Award for it!*

Pedro in
The Last of Us

Pedro was nominated for many awards, or prizes, for *The Last of Us*. He won the People's Choice Award for male TV star of the year! When the second season of the show came out in 2025, Pedro continued to wow fans as Joel.

ICONIC!

More than 8 million people watched the ***finale*** *of season one of* The Last of Us*!*

THE LAST OF US
HBO max

Making Movies

In 2024, Pedro starred in two blockbuster movies. He voiced a fox named Fink in *The Wild Robot*. Then, he played General Acacius in *Gladiator II*. Pedro had to train really hard for all the fighting he did in the movie!

ICONIC!

Pedro had trained with swords before, especially when he did **Game of Thrones*****. He took his skills to another level for*** **Gladiator II*****!***

Pedro in Gladiator II

Part of a Team

In February 2024, Marvel Studios announced that Pedro would be playing "Mister Fantastic" Reed Richards in *The Fantastic Four: First Steps* in 2025. Not only that, Pedro would play this part in other upcoming Marvel movies. This icon has only just begun his rise!

ICONIC!

Pascal has said that being part of The Fantastic Four *was something he couldn't say no to!*

Timeline

1975	*Pedro Pascal is born.*
1993-1997	*He goes to New York University.*
1999	*He first appears on TV.*
2014	*He appears on* Game of Thrones.
2015	Narcos *comes out.*
2019	The Mandalorian *comes out.*
2023	*Pedro begins starring in* The Last of Us.
2024	*He stars in* The Wild Robot *and* Gladiator II.
2025	The Fantastic Four: First Steps *comes out.*

For More Information

BOOKS

Beecroft, Simon, et al. *Star Wars Character Encyclopedia.* New York, NY: DK Publishing, 2024.

National Geographic Society (U.S.), ed. *Weird but True! Star Wars*. Washington, DC: National Geographic, 2024.

WEBSITE

Marvel Movies

https://www.marvel.com/movies

Check out some of the movies Pedro has coming out as Mister Fantastic.

Pedro Pascal IMDb

https://www.imdb.com/name/nm0050959/

Follow Pedro's career here.

Publisher's note to educators and parents: Our editors have carefully reviewed these websites to ensure that they are suitable for students. Many websites change frequently, however, and we cannot guarantee that a site's future contents will continue to meet our high standards of quality and educational value. Be advised that students should be closely supervised whenever they access the internet.

Glossary

audition: Tryout.

career: A job someone chooses to do for a long time.

finale: The end of something.

iconic: Having to do with being well established.

nominate: To suggest someone for an honor.

opportunity: A good chance for progress.

perform: To carry out an action, such as acting or playing music.

professional: Having to do with something someone gets paid to do.

resolve: To decide firmly.

showrunner: Someone who oversees the making of a TV show.

Index